SPLAKE

t. kilgore splake

Transcendent Zero Press

Houston, Texas

ISBN-13: 978-0996270441
ISBN-10: 0996270442

Library of Congress Control Number: 2015959470

Printed in the United States of America

16429 El Camino Real Apt. 7
Houston, TX 77062

Cover Design: Glenn Monroe Irby

FIRST EDITION

Transcendent Zero Press

SPLAKE

t. kilgore splake

I have published poetry collections since 2013 under my press imprint Transcendent Zero Press, although I felt the tug of poetry in my DNA when I first penned love poems to teenage crushes and tributes to family who cared for me.

I can say with a straight face authors recognized in this splake collection have not impressed me of late. I read Kerouac and the Beats in my high school years and studied *Mexico City Blues* carefully, making notes in the margins as I am sure poets are wont to do. I have fond memories of Kerouac, especially his novels, but I sometimes think he is overrated. I feel Ginsberg is the superior poet.

I have never approached Brautigan, but Hemingway's *The Old Man and the Sea* I read alongside Cervantes and Didion during my sophomore year in high school — by force of the curriculum. Perhaps I did not meet Hemingway's best face. Bukowski is truly the working class author of grit, and in one of his posthumous collections he jokes that he threw a Hemingway book in the trash because he couldn't write. This was Bukowski's early judgment after buying a book in a gift shop during Hemingway's blooming years.

I later read *From Whom the Bell Tolls*, a book my grandmother owned even though she frequently called Hemingway a narcissist. This is a word more often than not thrown at authors one finds disagreeable, too introverted, perhaps egoistic or self-affirming.

The word narcissist is awfully fashionable. It is so easy to attach psychological complexes to cultural figures — in fact, Churchill hasn't avoided psychoanalysis so why should his inferiors? In his essay collection *Kafka's Mice*, psychoanalyst Anthony Storr picks the brains of great leaders and artists to find a deep seated sense of slight and inferiority present in them. However, each living soul is tormented in some capacity.

In splake's collection of poems, many tributes to heroes and others that celebrate living simply are present — there is also the eternal 'I am, and ask for no explanation'. splake does not coddle the reader like a baby, sugarcoating lust with spiritualizing. He affirms life and he seeks a higher order in simplicity and defies the usual authorities with spark and courage.

splake began his writing career during a drunken evening in front of a campfire with a single poem. It is in the moment he decides to stop teaching and withdraw into the woods. We can find other comparisons in American literature, such as Henry David Thoreau who tested the tenets of the Transcendentalist credo. Hemingway could find a trace of his ideal in splake's lifestyle. I have read multiple splake collections and find his style sheared of the glitter some poetry adds for decoration, and his lines are impressionistic and direct. He is playing photographer or manic observer.

Where do we place his poetry in the American tradition? At this moment, tradition isn't all that matters. Let's look to its future for a true vision of its merits. Nietzsche wrote that the present not only contains the past, but the future. Live a moment like it is configured to create the next moment, and think of Fate as your harsh mistress. We have poems of wilderness, poems of historical fact, and poems that reveal the inner workings of a man's curiosity of woman. We have poems of time and place, and poems that are based on anecdote, or writing that celebrates wisdom.

I especially love "poem for alastor" and its rich simplicity. Poetry weaves image and voice with wisdom and recollection, and this poem is certainly a fine model.

Try these lines for your palate:

> "hey, will you look at the old guy with the huge gray beard, man
>
> his skin must be tough as an old alligator hide, sure takes his time
>
> hiking down the road, wonder where he lives,"

This poem is ultimately about the future being of its author—splake himself is set to haunt the woods, since he knows them well.

Of course, we could accuse splake of fearless narcissism for his courage to see himself through the eyes of others. But we won't.

With print-on-demand, there are huge numbers of budding authors who plan to hit the big time. With a tiny minority of self-published writers actually collecting decent royalties, it is dubious that one is special in this expanding milieu. Anyone with a thumb and forefinger nimble enough to hold a pen can publish a book with a few clicks. This is great news because now we have literary democracy with everyone chipping in their best attempts. There is the sad fact that the market is saturated with books that no one will buy, and this saturation implies the worthy collections are often lost to consideration. With more books in print, there is more competition. We should praise the market's opening for creating avenues so authors can live their dreams, but we should also be realistic in our understanding of market dynamics. I am one to say, "The more, the merrier!" However, print books seem out of style since the invention of ebooks. Barnes and Noble now have an entire space for ebook readers. Brick and mortar stores are fighting to take royalties from authors to keep alive, proving that technology is killing face-to-face contact. Everything is a button click and a doorbell ring ahead of you.

Let's not get hasty and assume the book is dead, that poetry is passé. Poetry is vital. People still quote poems and ask for poetry at special occasions. *And there was a time when bad poetry got performers decapitated.* In the United States, Rumi is widely appreciated. Libraries open visitors to all, and I sometimes see middle-agers in the poetry section taking a glance at the latest collections. Poet laureate spaces are opening up all over the country, from city to state level. Poetry may not make poets wealthy celebrities, but it is a force of healing and the poet as healer will never leave us. Poetry is a spiritual energy that harmonizes the reader's perceptions and thoughts. When we are open to poetry, it best works its magic.

It is odd though how many poets are closet self-haters. With hearts abounding in love of creation, why do poets alone suffer this malady so severely? Thank the God who created Nature for bringing editors into being. Otherwise, not a single poetry book would withstand superficial inspection.

Small presses are a surging trend in poetry publishing, and the independent literary scene is flourishing widely. In my home city of Houston, Texas, there is a gathering every night of the week somewhere to celebrate poetry. If your city isn't recognizing poetry, open a space at a local store or find a park and get a gathering going.

However, I notice a tendency occurring that shouldn't in the literary scene. Poets are naturally friendly and accepting, and we should avoid cliqueishness. Many scenes break into small factions and only one group or another are expected to certain types of performance. One group hangs at the coffeehouse, and another at the bookstore. This is not intended to be like high school where the cool kids hang at the street corner and the outliers in the cafeteria. Poets break boundaries!

The time is ripe for the written word — we have avenues open to us, but we have to make them bloom. Widen your sphere of influence, buy more independent poetry collections, think outside of your box and challenge others. Buy a book published by a small press you adore and make a gift of it to a friend. Share poetry with everyone. Write in greeting cards, mail poetry fliers, and start a critique circle! Go out!

I hope you enjoy this collection by t. kilgore splake. Poetry collections are a huge labor of love. The satisfaction I have in it is the enjoyment you find.

introduction

in reviewing my past writings, i have found there was a strong masculine influence in my thinking and literary reflections. the works of hemingway, bukowski, ed abbey, and albert huffstickler have been very important to my writing. initially, i did not relate to the "beat writers", but after a short while, i quickly learned to appreciate the writings of kerouac, ginsberg, corso, ferlinghetti, and others. however, my favorite poet is richard brautigan, and i particularly enjoyed the wit and humor found in his earlier books.

beside my spiritual center in the cliffs and finding much comfort alone in the wilderness, i also have an early morning coffee habit. my current coffee drinking place in calumet is the rosetta café. last spring, shoe music press published a collection of my espresso poems titled "rosetta café".

my poetry writings are in the lower case, as editor jim chandler once said, i didn't miss the need of a big ego push with my work. my earlier poems used the left margin for their literary format, while in more recent writings, i have chosen to center my works. the current splake poems reflect a more spartan style than the more detailed works of my first writings.

contents

about the author

in real life, i am margaret smith's favorite son, tom. however, my creative identification is t. kilgore splake.

many summers ago while camping in the pictured rocks outback in michigan's upper peninsula, i suddenly began writing poetry. this was when i realized that all of my life i had been a poet and was waiting for the moment to happen. like doris lessing said after she started writing, i felt as if my real life was beginning.

the summer that i started writing poetry, i caught a trophy fish called a splake. also, that same summer i read all of the dell press kurt vonnegut paperback books. so, while seeking an adequate nom-de-plume, i added my splake to vonnegut's character kilgore trout from his book "breakfast of champions". the result was t. kilgore splake and the rest is american literary history.

in 1989, the state of michigan granted me an early retirement from my college teaching position at kellogg community college in battle creek, michigan. for ten years, i lived in the michigan upper peninsula village of munising. i "learned" about writing by putting words on paper and without any formal literary rules, or the influence of mfa demands. i lack sympathy with others who "talk" about a new work, but never get around to writing it. also, i feel the litmus test of a poet is not his work, but his next poem.

after working and writing in munising for ten years i moved farther north to calumet, michigan, and for many years lived above the omphale art gallery. shortly after settling in calumet, i discovered the old cliffs mining site located north of the village. the cliffs have provided me a sacred place to visit. I

regularly climb the cliffs and reflect up on my recent writings as well as "think out" new creative projects to pursue. on each of my cliffs treks i keep a careful eye open for my mysterious mountain lion friend.

acknowledgements

it is important to me to mention several people who have provided me with valuable assistance for my writings and publications.

eric greinke and roseanne ritzeman of *presa press* have helped me greatly with their editing and publishing of several splake books. alison vyain, editor of *moon publishing and printing*, has published many of my poems and photographs in her literary magazine, "the moon". she has also produced three splake chapbooks. gordon purkis, editor of *shoe music press,* has published splake books and selected many of my poems for his literary journal, "penny ante feud". i have forgotten how many benefits jim chandler, editor of *thundersandwich press,* has provided me. jim and i cooperated in the creation of several splake books.

also, i am deeply in debt to the late dave christy, editor of *alpha beat press*, as well as the fine literary input from dave church who recently passed away. in addition, i received serious and solid literary parsing from scot young, editor of *rusty truck press*, robert zoschke, editor of *the lowdown*, and paul bach jr.

early wilderness poems

early morning dance

hiking boots skipping through the mists
down winding forest path, pausing to lick
tiny sweet beads of last evening's rain off
soft fresh leaves,
leaving a trail of haiku pinned on trees
poetry etched on winter-hardened oak
leaves, ink of ripe red berries, unashamed
verse a moment among willing woodland ears,
then blending back in rich soft loess.

ice out

many afternoons of tall hot sun melts lake
ice and floes, swelling small streams to turgid
force, slowly swimming, roe fat belly circling
warm tides, husbanding heavy breaths behind
tender pink slits, a fishy ooze protecting tiny
silver scales, finally drawn past furious delta
currents, mysterious passion, upstream, wetness
sliding over many spring deadfall snags, energy
spent moving past beaver dams again and again,
at last in quiet headwater safety having bested
lamprey, otter, black bear predators, releasing
blood orange eggs on sparkling gravel spit, rolling
unsteady in silent eddies, unable to stay upright

a soft palm caresses damp sweaty braids, bruised
lips lightly touch, a low whisper, "you know, love,
they die from the slightest touch."

dream kill

nervous fingers and
unsteady eye narrow down a lead bead, in
silent aftershock soft brown fur lies steaming
in gray early mists, tearing open its chest,
devouring the heart, saving the liver for later
sustenance on our long odyssey, crawling
inside between mahogany stained ribs for
sanguine warmth, needing his clear eyes and
sharp scent for flight back to tribal hogans, the
times of great feasts, abundant eagle feathers
and pelts, fat fish bellies smoking, visiting in
dead of winter the indian "shamans" around
flickering fires, carving grotesque blood
tortured faces from flat antler bones, back to a
beginning when sweet luscious fish would soon
leave fossil lines in white coral along red and
golden gravels of great lake shores.

poem for alastor

> alastor — androgynous half-spirit
> half man who lived in the woods and
> worshipped intellectual beauty

hey, will you look at the old guy with the huge gray beard, man
his skin must be tough as an old alligator hide, sure takes his time
hiking down the road, wonder where he lives,

you ever meet him, what is he really like, where the hell did he come from,
understand he retired after too many years and students in some small
downstate classroom, lost a wife and about the same time, rumors
that he was a talented writer, a poet it seems, but for some reason quit,

now spends all his time trout fishing, has all the "topos" between grand
marais and melstrand memorized, stored in his brain, they say there's
no rainbow hole or beaver dam brookie pond he doesn't know about,

april he sets up camp somewhere and lives off the trout he catches, uses
vegetables from a garden hidden in the woods, moving on to new pond
or stream section when fishing turns poor, lives this way until the end of
october and it really turns cold,

folks think there's an old trailer out near ross lake where he catches stuff,
rice, hooks, line, clearing for a small garden, where he leans in for the
winter,

every time i see him moseying down the road or across the plains i get a bit jealous, fresh trout, cooked rice, spring vegetables and sassafras tea isn't exactly a crazy way of life, eh,

one day soon he'll have to pick a single trout stream and become a ghost waiting to surprise those who wander into his camp.

t. kilgore splake

<u>winter prayer</u>

oh lord,

                                may bright warm sun
beams continue to green the spring forest, blossom
the beautifully colored woodland wildflowers, and
bleach my gray beard red,

                              please, one more time

hemingway

<u>old train station</u>
<u>seney michigan</u>

the film was fresh, camera setting correct
and still my print contained unexplained
dark shadows,
       hiding the apparition
of an earlier visitor returned too late to
stalk the twin-hearted trout again, his
grasshopper bait in a glass bottle hanging
from his neck

<u>micro-wave fishsticks</u>

"papa"
  afternoon soaps
  puke tube humming
  waiting cartoon reruns
  graying brook trout
  dozing
  tag alder shadows

darger frame "papa"

henry escaping

illinois asylum for feeble-minded

walking to chicago

janet surviving

electro-shock therapy

clinical lobotomy solution

old hem

early mornings watching

sawtooth mountain ghosts

three writers

facing empty page

patiently waiting

one true sentence

papa

"... he was a hopeless alcoholic with a seriously
confused personality and a malignant streak for
self-destruction. on july 2, 1961, just like the
great marlin he so loved to reel in, he went belly
up."

the detroit news, 1/22/89

what would critics want, ernest returning from the "great
war" in suit, white shirt, tie, teaching junior high english,
diagramming sentences, worrying about crab grass, sneaking
off to the oak park vfw saturday afternoons for a beer,

or literary notoriety before retirement, dusty niche in
some big ten faculty, trotted out, halftime at fall football
games, on display like stuffed wolverine or spartan,

finally leaving his brain to menninger clinic, body
on exhibit at ketchum historical society, cojonnes in large pickle
jar for the customers at "sloppy joe's" in key west,

maybe the final act was really courageous foresight,
backed against the sawtooth mountains, savvy bull seeing the
sword behind the cape, wise old lion, trophy bluefish, sensing
the xx express charge, razor sharp barbs clinching deep,

what poet or romantic can think of a hard, gritty paris
rain, light breezes cooling serengeti savannah, tides pulsing
warm caribbean "gulf stream", rainbows rising to hatch on
big two-hearted, without imagining a joyful, testy ghost of
papa,

warhol declared life a fifteen minute run, and ernie
played to a chorus of oles for a long count fourteen, a helluva
"afternoon in the sun", before the second slowly disappeared
in corrida dust.

<u>hunter</u>

soft spring paris showers, with soulmate hadley, safe
sawmill apartment sanctuary and retreat, open windows, air
full of wetness, aromas of bedroom sex,

roasted coffee flavors, crusty fresh bread bakery scents
sweet, rich croissant breakfasts,

noisy music-dance hall revelry, after writing days went
well, hanging out, drinking with sailors, whores, expat others
playing at being artists,

saving little magazines, newspapers checks for picnics
and race track respites, late spring schruns alpine runs,
renting cheap pamplona posada, running with bulls,
watching primo toreadors,

26

hem's long lonely hours, silently writing, worrying, stray gypsy dog companion on walks to shakespeare and company, browsing, chatting with alice and gertrude,

sacrificing the good life, first true love to kill, slay mighty gulf stream marlins, murder magnificent african rhinos, elephants, full brace of canadian northerns, continuously chasing his black inner angers,

hunkering down behind sawtooths, hiding in dark shadows, exhausted "papa", too weary for new dramatics, unable to write,

begging for mercy, asking help passing through darkness, waiting on souls, those wasted with no reverence, spirits, returning to take revenge

paris memories

hemingway's
saw mill apartment
notre-dames-des-champs
one decent suit
respectable pair of shoes
generation perdue
lost generation poet
not trusting non-veterans
deux magots *café au lait*
zinc bar cheap vino
seeking one true sentence
another and another
talking with seine fishermen
angling *goujon* dinner
horse chestnut rabbit's foot
good luck charm
disciplined schedule
born to create books
hating wasted days
empty notebook pages
"pilot fish and rich"
ruining *a moveable feast*
best place to work
with everyday fiestas
collecting lazy friends
while searching for new place
schruns mountain lodge

winter skiing vacation

hadley's stolen suitcase

gare de lyon station

short stories gone

life moving on

love marrying

pauline martha mary

spanish civil war

battle of hurtgen forest

african safaris

hunting wild animals

open veldt expanse

fishing gulf stream currents

pilar sailfish days

old man and the sea

floridita "papa dobles"

finca working retreat

"city of lights"

final chapter

sawtooth mountain shadows

silence solitude writing

young hem wisdom, obscure writer, poet during early paris days,

before idolized "papa," abortive "dangerous summer," on road to
ketchum via mayo clinic,

living above sawmill near ezra's flat, noise driving him to small hotel
writing room, nearby rue,

daily paying literary dues before browsing shakespeare's book titles,
trading writing gossip with sylvia, gertrude before savoring late afternoon
vino,

avoiding street bistro phonies, rummy boulevard poseurs, who believe
talking the same as doing,

same as today's kerouac pretenders, television "talking heads," devout
twelve-steppers, divine born-agains, eager to describe tomorrow's
masterpiece.

explosion over ketchum

"what is life? it is the breath of the buffalo in the
 wintertime, it is the flicker of the firefly in the night,
 it is the little shadow that runs across the fields and
 loses itself in the sunset."

native american wisdom

january darkness, "whoo/hoo, whoo/hoo screech echoing
down salmon river, floating across the snow valleys of lost
river range, raptors haunting harbinger telling ernie the dance is
finished, time for one last kiss, then vanish,

papa's soul soaring on chilly evening ethers, ghost speeding
the miles back home, safely hidden by clouds, masking moon's
shadows,

back to big two-hearted river, trading mountain wisdom for
trout wisdom, bedding down in hollow old pine left over from
logging era, waiting out february, the month of doubt,

calm specter like silent deer, in timeless sanctuary, unbothered
by mosquitoes, blackfly hoards, camping below remote beaver dam
on flooded muskeg meadow,

plump brookies, ospreys, bitterns for companions, occasional rogue black bear passing through, brush hawks riding tall warm thermals, watching shine of wolf's eyes during evening lightning storm,

peaceful solitude, warm summer winds gently rustling leaves, pine needles, memories of bacon grease, condensed milk, apple butter and onion sandwiches,

abandoning deep swamp darkness, glass bottle of grasshoppers, mysterious "big fish," hurtgen forest terrors, worries over chicago novel,

if things get boring, papa can mosey down the river, check out seney, find wise old lady at andy's, enjoy wild and exciting big two-hearted weekend.

poet

early morning

shaking off zzzz's

tossing couchin' it blankets

toes sticking out of

holes in red socks

graybeard artist

bard 'res' sanctuary

superman's

fortress of solitude

bat cave and blackhawk's island

escapist's "key hole"

under empire state building

rice madness stew

cooling in crockpot

hot plate turkey legs warming

shredded bran-wheat squares

spoon sized snack

basic bardic diet

without salt sugar fat

solitary scribe

beyond true romance

leaving love to movies

poontang desires

memories of past lifetimes

viagra "blue bomber"

waiting for smart

mature knowing woman

twenty-one year old tranny

ancient dodge la strata

steady dependable wheels

no wild dreams

classy lamborghini

small mind plaything

reclusive rogue

not giving a damn

never traveling

seeing different places

meeting other people

instead leaving society

to know-nothing pretenders

those watching tv soap operas

sit-com reruns

late nights

trickster coyote hunter

chasing dangerous prey

brain-skull cavity imaginations

measuring existential conflicts

lightness darkens

in real world contests

no more alcoholic courage

zanax lexapro valium help

writer's block excuses

regardless of serotonin levels

testosterone and dark rainy

far northern dreariness

daily wresting elusive

damn dame lady muse

writing new

poems and stories

tommy splake smith

dream book manuscript

early winter mornings

climbing cliffs

warm wool watch cap

snug against ears

welcome witness to cool

salmon-violet sunrise

now and then

leaning into clippers

fresh buzzzzz-job

pushing back pale beard

yearly near-terminal

spring motorcycle fevers

always surviving

daily metros post grabbery

mailbox incomings

waiting new netflix film

next ammo-zon

single-click book order

always knowing if cubs won

how celts did

new york giants michigan wolverines

game time scores

once laughing at him

now thinking papa was right

life and poetry

should be damn straight

fox river odyssey with nick adams

tried the question a couple of times in seney, "anyone around who
still remembers when ernest hemingway jumped out of the
boxcar for a fishing trip, and made the fox fiver the 'big two-
hearted' of literary fame,"

one spring steve at the mobilgas said "the old sob probably
just came and stayed drunk for a week, slept under the bridge
never wetting a line, then went back to the newspaper and made
up his fish story,

next spring, steve's son agreed that this was probably true, so,
i decided to roam around the fox headwaters, fish, look around,
and not try to find out,

at first dawn light drove an aging bronco torturous miles of
winding two-wheel ruts, eventually sliding a canoe down wet
grasses to pond waters, scattering nesting sandhill cranes, also
disturbing a beaver family slapping their tails making a hasty
retreat,

fast rising sun burning off cool morning mists, drying icy
beads in spider webs, black flies constantly hovered, biting clouds
of mosquitoes an endless swarm, around a pond dogleg,
portaging two ancient beaver dams, finally arriving at flooded
muskeg meadow of river meanders, one plump brookie already in
creel,

large brown fish hawk lazily circling as the high noon sun
baked hot against welts rising from my neck, when i saw nick,
shadowy figure resting under some second growth pines in the
distance, where marsh grass turned to upland soils,

trace of bacon grease and streak of dried condensed milk still
in his beard, apple butter pancake and onion sandwich lunch set
before him, laughing at me,

greenhorn trout fisherman furiously grasping at small willow
bushes, ass and billfold valuables soaked by sudden icy plunge,
finally pulling free of sinkhole ooze, cold shock and reminder of
tragedy waiting the unwary alone in the woods, nick mocking the
foolish who fish during hot noon when high sky and bright sun
make trout wary,

temptation to wave, holler adams down to chat, tell fishing
lies, smoke, but quickly recall, he did not like to fish "with other
men,"

so i left him to the bitterns high up among the pine, cedar, and
birch trees, let him have his dreamy nap, knowing later when
dark purple clouds turn to dusk,

with bottle of grasshoppers around his neck, flour sack tied to
waist, he will climb over the log pile, amid cool night shadows,
this time working the "big fish," playing sandy pebbles and gravel
further this time, maybe even into the swamp.

bukowski

hank

trickster rascal chinaski, tough guy, three fisted boozer,
cover for real softie, truly loved his women, attached man,
quietly sentimental,

realizing empty sex of bodies numbers game, another score,
searching woman to get close to, lost in her soul's passions,
finding warm place in lady's heart,

certain abused, hardened personas could be renewed,
become loving if they sincerely believed,

sleazo rental rooms, old beater tranny, shoes, socks, with
holes, dead end jobs to buy food, booze, typing paper, pay for
little daughter marina's ice cream treats,

providing new definition to "survivor," said young teen,
without high school prom date, determined to have his dance,
find love,

like jeffers, hemingway, the other lost, silent poets "who
almost made it" before becoming old, running out of time

chinaski

imagine hank getting his high school senior prom date
falling in love marrying young,

house beautiful mortgage, worrying about crabgrass,
dandelions, nervous about what the neighbors might be saying,

fathering children, quickly mastering dad's power of
manipulation, withholding love from wife, daughters, sons,

how long before discovering "nada" life, achy void at center
of his "self", hearing thundering refrain of bellow's henderson,
deafening "i wanti wanti want",

making drunken hard-on escape, fleeing middle class
snobbery, pious posturings, cheap slum rooms, driving old
junkers, used lot "specials", wearing shoes, socks with holes,
eating once a day,

difficult economizing to buy booze, pens, paper, pay postage
to send his stories to magazine editors, finally discovering
magic of fine classical music, "ten win a comfortable bet,
wisdom writing with brutal honesty, hank's holiness telling the
truth

t. kilgore splake

looking for chinaski's bar

went with friend into mexico looking for cantina where
charley drank regularly, i'd been there once before, but old
"t-town" streets a maze, many unmarked walls and doors,
people with some sort of business going in and out,

drank there once with mexicana girlfriend, plain, well lit
cantina, but not clean inside, blue-collar amigo-types drank
in small clusters along the bar, muy beer, primo heavy
smooth taste like cream ale and spit,

friend wearied so we hiked back toward the border
through shadowy calles, out of the shadows, a borracho,
hollered "fucking americans", as we pushed past his
slumped body,

should have asked if he knew old cantina we were
looking for, if he might have known bukowski,

opportunities lost, even for a couple of gringos, dusty
dark tijuana alleys,

charley would have been saddened

weekend existentials

saturday morning racing into early sunday, "carmina burana" soft dull hum, nerves raw, wired from all day espresso, second day of fresh de-tox try, empty brown bottles scattered around like squad of motley soldiers at ease, shower nozzle steady drip-drip-dripping, toilet gurgling, water clear, thinking "jesus, didn't i just put in a new blue bowl cleaner pellet a couple of days ago," kitchen counter collection of empty styrene coffee cups, "rice madness stew" crockpot with three months of stains, wild karmic accumulation, something for later ancient study, aging canon typewriter with broken metal plug, machine has to be jiggled in order to work, fucking state-of-the-arts technology developing a mind of its own, cheap-ass quill typer ribbons flaking black ink, liftoffs leaving white correction "ghosts", brain-skull cavity whispering sweetness of .357 lollypop, sudden nighttime noise, windy rustlings from black outside, blowing front door open a bit, thinking, "ah, old hank and his bmw passing, taking a shortcut home to california, after visiting friends, lovely women out east, already i am beginning to feel better.

charles bukowski's lost daughter

famous creative father always someplace else, psychic break, emotional meltdown between early teen birthday, bleak christmas season,

trading virginity at thirteen for real good dope, crazy nam vet with gonorrhea, black nightmare flashbacks,

certain polite mannered men weak, settling for least threatening, abusive relationships with not too wacky guys,

coked up boyfriend mad over no sex staining next morning's job interview dress with cum, her sad whispers, i was beginning to trust you,

butt raped, beaten by three arabs, expensive chicago suite, tossed out on the street, no purse, suitcase, clothes, bad pale dog miles back home, watching dark bruises turning yellow,

store front clinic "meds", in between sanitarium shock treatments, jacking prescription doses around so just a little bit crazy, days spent toking, filling notebooks with scribbled poetry, heavy-metal phone plugged in her brain, learning she was dysfunctional and lacking necessary socialization from afternoon talk shows,

discovering self-esteem through cruelty, power-trip fucking "bad boys", old men affairs, calling them "daddy", greedy gift grabber until they became boring,

vodka-tranq breakfasts, bottle and a half into the day, chain smoking, word salad stream of consciousness early morning telephone marathons, maybe "suicide today" before declaring "let's party" with little-girl-childish delight,

binge junk food orgies, anorexic mood swings, pink bedroom walls, singing to dolls, teddy bear, school pictures of daughter alea living upstate with grandmother

shoplifting sprees, boosting cheap knicky-knacks, quick adrenalin rush, later throwing stuff away, stopping in for mission free meal, coffee,

welfare this and special aid that, food stamps, surplus commodities, no clue on next moth's rent, beater tranny down, no money for insurance, repairs

t. kilgore splake

arrested drug house bust, two days "angel dust" withdrawals before "tanked out" on bail, little alea in social services custody, temporary foster family stay,

angry hatreds making hard young girl gritty, "don't hurt, don't care" survivor, believing society, somebody owes her,

sneaking past iron cemetery gate late nights, stripping naked, shadows hiding botched abortion scars, fleshy wrinkles of no longer young body, fingers massaging dry vagina folds, weeping "dad, goddamn you charlie, why did you keep me waiting, why, why, why,"

moist early dampness soaking tree bark, stone marker, withered flowers, vase, loose leaf notebook, wrinkled pages of poems, sliver of moon dissolving slowly into pale first dawn,

broken heart of a little girl once long ago, now sad, growing cold like distant burned-out star trailing across heavens before disappearing.

kerouac

t. kilgore splake

<u>kerouac sur</u>

pillow darkness
mouth to mouth
kiss to kiss

<u>madness</u>

kerouac
looking for fires
desolation peak summer
seeking angelic beatitude
sterling cooper ad men
don roger peter
selling america
things they don't need
waiting christmas bonus

big sur death

sad desperate jack
drinking cheap red wine
fighting darkness
daily escaping madness
somehow surviving nights
zen sutras empty
catholic wisdom failing
fearing mother not waiting
never writing again

wannabe

non-artistic voice
criticizing other poets
their words describing
"contempt of man"
retreating to safe
bible mother flag apple pie
girlfriend's silky sedge
no *on the road*
sal and dean miles
looking for answers

<u>holy road</u>

no more
on the road
ballin' the jack
following white-line fevers
dancing master death's
beat declaration
nada mas
zooming all night miles
neal's "it"
lost in shadows

kerouac in the cliffs

goddammit jack goddammit
squeeze last drop
of cheap red port
time for new spiritual adventure
not escaping san francisco
to ferlinghetti's cabin
california's big sur canyon
instead turning miles
north to calumet
facing cliffs granite heights
crossing brautigan creek
waters holding many secrets
careful steps to summit
occasionally pausing
for wild thimbleberry feast
slaking thirst at seep
shafts of sunlight
filtering through foliage
lighting forest shadows
foggy mornings
lighthouse horn
warning lake superior ships
no big sur burro
maybe mountain lion
or rogue deer watching
cliffs soils
slit from history's glaciers
ancient indians

early copper miners
out traveling ghosts
still running away
fleeing madness
cliffs some place new
forgetting youthful dreams
realizing future is now
maybe last chance
to save your ass

beat road benison

v-e day, v-j day, "ti jean," 50s generation, small mill
towns across america, watching spring rivers rising, flood
tides sweeping under bridges, waters flowing to other places,
an outside world,

late black nights, alarm clock's existential tick-tocking
growing louder, gunshot explosions deafening, racing
heartbeat, pulse,

restless young boys weary of school routines, classroom,
teacher demands, chafing at obedience to "thou shalt nots,"
arid conformity, tortured american puritan ethic,

everyday classes, homework, football practices, games,
friday night record music sock hops, school gym, hanging
out, lunch wagon, dairy bar, poolroom haunts,

estranged father relations, rejecting their greasy
mechanic's hands, tired mill worker hours, suit, white shirt,
tie, 9 to 5 undesirable agenda, alien territory,

pouty, teeny-voiced miniature blonde madonna-
mary girlfriends, going steadies, tiny titties beneath tight
soft sweaters, young teenage boys still mother's heroes,
gabrielles, margarets, continuous talk about going to college,
getting an education they couldn't understand,

confusing, contrasting, colliding ideologies, capitalism,
americanism, christianism, communism, political right, left,
platforms, party proposals, clouding the brain, complex
country, international problems without easy answers, no
immediate quick solutions,

small towns fighting decay, slow gradual death, trees
fallen, feeding "build, build, build" fevers, new home sites
for future nelson, anderson, cleaver families, sears and
roebuck house beautiful america, madison avenue's constant
message "buy buy buy" more stuff dreams,

young men growing disenchanted wondering "is this all
there is," in a hurry for real life to begin, eager to prowl,
roam, do something other than please pious, ignorant
small-town coaches, priests, policemen, off to see the big
city, make it, become a real all-american man,

new york city, "village" bohemian and poet hanging out with others talking art, antler booths, white horse tavern

tables, browsing coliseum and strand bookstores for used paperback bargains, perusing new poetry chapbooks on gotham shelves, cheap spaghetti dinners, smoky basement italian cafes, stubby candles flickering, dripping wax down empty chianti bottles' wicker coverings, lively exciting washington square, collection of small theaters, clubs, white castle hamburgers, beautiful young women, arty girls dressed in tight black clothes, long bouncy ponytails,

> " . . . you touch me i hear the
> sound of mandolins . . . with your
> kiss my life begins . . . you're
> spring to me, all things to me . .
> . darling cling to me, for we
> arecreatures of the wind, and
> wild is the wind. "

creative young artist minds, eisenhower 1950s in rebellion, rejecting commercialism, opposing unthinking, lockstep conformity to marriage, children, home, swimming pool, lawn to mow, television, popcorn, ice cream, pizza, family movie weekends, sunday church services and sermons, lone metropolitan exile, cruel, demanding quiet long hours writing poems, plays, books, staring down the ominous blank page, in serious contest with damned dame muse, creating stories, characters, sal paradise, ray smith, cody pomeray, dean moriarty, japhy ryder, richard wisp, adam yulch, moving literary dreams,

> *"i'm looking for that lonely*
> *street, i've got a sad, sad*
> *tale to tell . . . perhaps to*
> *find someone to bandy*
> *broken dreams and watch*
> *an old love die . . . a lonely*
> *street where dim lights*
> *bring forgetfulness, where*
> *broken dreams and*
> *memories meet, ... "*

in between successes, failures, literary scores, rejections, route 66, the great "mother road" inviting highway miles road-rapture-odyssey west, short pacific coast, san francisco stay and sojourn, listening to ginsberg read "howl", wildly declaring himself and others "beat", with loose collection of writer-poet friends, snyder, corso, rexroth, creeley, burroughs, joyce johnson, "huncky", sam and ann charters, the city lights bookstore, awakened on dark early new york city morning, wild subterranean rumblings below concrete pavement, deep in earthen core, another detox failure, hincty to ninth degree, feeling madness closing in, night terror flashback hallucinations, north atlantic, surviving icy torpedo death, primal crushing scream rising "what am i doing here,"

"you made me leave my happy
home, you took my love and
now you're gone . . . i get the
blues about every night since i
fell for you"

feeling a vision from cody, "yes, it's time to go home, yes, home, home," seek the new, final satori, get well on big sur bluffs above the pacific, aboard a pale dog west, nerved on black coffee, a few johnny walker "reds" past noon, rucksack library, dostoevsky, flaubert, baudelaire, rimbaud, mike hammer paperback, bag of white castle hamburgers, off to chi-town, catch the zephyr, rails, big wheels rolling across the plains, prairies, deserts, west, whooee,

"stop the world and let me
off, i'm tired of going
round and round, i've
played the game of love
and lost, oh stop the
world and let me off."

diesel fume nausea, square wheels bounce, turning over lonely concrete miles through america's "heartland of pure thinking," passing through settlements of wasp practicality, new jersey, pennsylvania, ohio, indiana metes and bounds, deep yoga breaths hoping to clear static ricocheting around the skull, praying the d.t.s don't return, staring past bus bound window, looking for elwood, his rabbit "wild one" brando, big harley growling, robert mitchum in his ill-fated last run,

> *" . . . though a candle burned*
> *at both ends can never last out*
> *the night, harlem butterfly it*
> *makes a lovely light, a lovely*
> *light."*

drifting, fitful dreaming, with thomasine again, black village girlfriend, playwright, poet, weekends, mad partying, blue note, vanguard cellar bands, listening to poets read, eagle café, harlem night club hopping with tommy, mingle with "jazz hipsters", early morning jam sessions, memories of sweet, soulful music like dope soothing, calming withdrawals, great riffs, chords and refrains, bix, "trane", mingus, the count, louis, "yardbird", diz, ornette, coleman hawkins, cool velvet "lady blues", "sassy sarah's" singing, village apartment breakfast feast, greasy omnibus ham, eggs, hash browns, black coffee menu, watching sun rise across new york skyline,

"an indigo tune sings to the
moon . . . refrain of a
lonesome lover . . . a moan
in blue that wails the long
night thru . . . of lonely
hearts to learn . . . of love
lost in harlem nocturne."

gary, hammond, cal city, east chicago, whiting, illinois state line, evergreen park, lake shore outer drive, polk, dearborn, street station boarded up, depot tower clock without hands, cabbie's "fuckin-a-right" to any trains west question, left curbside, alone, heavy rucksack load, ankles sore, swelling, near killing drink thirst, blank robot personas rushing past, stony "don't bother me" in hurrying faces,

shy solitary poet facing empty concrete miles, lonely road leading home and blessing benediction, knowing old highway bends and turns now a dangerous dark place, aware america's become a land of psychos, serial murderers, violent nightriders, spiritless flotsam and jetsam, now hard path, difficult odyssey to reach special dream vision,

thumb arched ready for travel, make the journey west, pretending to live inside a wild animal's heart, rogue grizzly, timber wolf, coyote, mountain lion borrowing its courage to pass alone through dark miles, distant perilous expanse, cicero, berwyn, lockport, joliet, wilmington,

bloomington, springfield, staunton, across the mississippi into missouri, quickly through metro st. louis ghetto, limits and miles and beyond,

> *road*
> *was slippery*
> *curve was sharp*
> *white robe, harp*
> *wings and harp*
> *"burma shave"*

lonely highway shoulder, quiet and empty lanes, no rides, no ghost cars from the past, grinning chrome grills, hudsons, studebakers, nashes, desotos, kaisers and fraziers, gone too vacation-bound station wagon touring families, weary husband-fathers, chilly ray-ban wife-mothers, backseat children rising from comic book stupor, "how many more miles" whiny chorus echo, americans all back home, maybe, washing cars, mowing lawns, barbecuing, worrying over crabgrass, dandelions, filling washers, loading dryers, kirkwood, eureka, st. clair, sullivan, cuba, st. james, rolla, waynesville, lebanon, springfield, joplin and out of old miss-our-i,

his face
was loved
by just his mother
he burma-shaved
and now—
oh brother

old rusting phillips 66 sign, cracked glass mobilgas globe, flying red horse wing shot wounded, hoping for a knockout beautiful woman caddy deville ridge and road romance, rock café chili, grannies hot beef sandwiches, club café deluxe baloney and cheese on rye, sweet pickles, potato chips, soda fountain mission orange, metro diner's "big bama pies", smoky anonymous bar and grill pink neon pause, quick old granddad snort, tap draft chaser, galena, baxter springs, quapaw, commerce, a few miles fast breath of kans-ass air,

the hobo
lets his
whiskers sprout
it's trains—not girls
that he takes out
burma-shave

into oklahoma and the oklahoma cities of the mind, loose telephone lines looped across listing poles, snaky wires flowing, lost in distant horizon, flat tires ringing fence posts, run down 4 tv channel motel, sad, tired furniture, clocks not working, vinta, claremore, sapulpa, bristow, ok city, clinton, sayre, dry dusty doomed roadside zoos, clothesline art and wares, cheap elvis, last supper prints, chenille spreads, robes, array of pottery, clay statues, rusty, empty water tanks distant silhouettes, desert scarecrows, imagining gray armies, ghostly immigrant arkies, okies, "joad" families of other depression hard times, fleeting glimpse, dillinger, bonnie and clyde, butch, sundance, jack london, lost orphan pony express boy wildly slapping leather, covered conestogas, settlers, relentless westward determination, outlaw "rio" russell, hem in ford coupe heading north to ketchum, with new wife,

> *he's the boy*
> *the girls forgot*
> *his line*
> *was smooth*
> *his chin was not*
> *burma-shave*

great state of tex-ass, jericho, groom, conway, old cowpoke rider spirits out roaming desert arroyos, arid barrancas, occasional "yee-haw" singing with gentle breezes, lone specter with distant stare, eyes burning like red hot coals, moonlight flooded skull, used to bedding down with bats, spiders, snakes, distant coyote companions, listening mournful nighttime plaints, old "bo's" waving hellos from empty boxcar doors, chessie cats traveling companions, steel rail, crosstie nomad ramblers, free men full of railroad fevers, irresistible lure, click-clacking metal wheels, brief pause, quaffing icy lone star longneck or three amarillo bar, pleasant chat with "chippy", gritty tough survivor, splendid on the road femme friend, washing away traveling dust, grit accumulations, telling a few lies before moving along,

"that big eight-wheeler
rolling down the track
means your true-loving
daddy ain't coming back,
cause i'm moving on, soon
i'll be gone . . . i'm moving
on."

tumcumcari, montoya, cuervo, santa rose, apache springs, pecos, santa fe, albuquerque, manuelito, late afternoon mauve-hued rocky mountains casting dark shadows, sudden trembling, hearing cody whisper "the dark laughter has come again, the dark laughter has come again," remembering the mad dash years ago, dharma bums climbing the mountain finally understanding the answer lies at the summit, knowing i've got to go away now, time to leave the road to others,

forget winona, miss old san berdoo, not make frisco city, the bookstores and poetry readings, time to cease being prisoner lost, trapped in mad fucking poem, no more racing starvation ridge to desolation "crackup", repeat sanitarium bars, lost months under heavy-duty medicines, haunted by dead father, memere, gerard, visions of jesus watching from his cross, unnecessary painful emotional burdens, declare freedom for football humiliations, sad "stardust", "tenderly", one and only high school love lost, inner angers, doubts, fears over new, next written word, impossible demands to be "hep, man, be hep", bedding down beside ancient pine scarred long ago by lightning, "wind-that-walks" breeze rustling needles, quiet humming, drinking nearby stream water cupped hands, slumber, warmed against deep night forest mists, dreaming of splendid mountain funeral stele, cairn, morning first light with ray, henry, george, alvah, cody, japhy, warren, again crossing the void once more, no longer afraid of altitude heights, hope for snow, must keep on climbing, higher and higher, above clouds now, climbing higher and higher, beyond.

brautigan

t. kilgore splake

<u>watermelon repair kit</u>

green adhesive tape

pink gauze underneath

imitation black seeds

might have saved brautigan

his watermelon sugars

slowly disappearing

finally running dry

<u>after the comma in my obituary</u>

plump rainbow

watermelon sugar

garlic "meats"

pumpkin tides

candlelions

marsha's

blonde beauty

a-plus

SPLAKE

trout angling odyssey

blue cloud
rum soaked "crooks"
keeping blackflies distant
pissing warm beer
streamside tall weeds
filling limit
without wetting line
bro brautigan magic

chairman

all but dissertation
npr and *new yorker* cartoons
pbs special features
unable to understand
brautigan stories and poems
"cleveland wrecking yard"
selling trout streams
five dollars a foot
while i laugh
wet happy tears

t. kilgore splake

brautigan score card

pumpkin tides

catfish friends

garlic meat ladies

absaroka summit

troll hut

vida

ianthe

"tfa shorty"

good talking candles

ideath

trout colored dreams

watermelon sugar

back window view

behind brautigan's hut

dusty path to village

beyond "forgotten works"

piney woods stream

flowing cold waters

plump beautiful trout

ideath

that mysterious bitch

our final

most sweetest love

richard's promise

she won't desert us

winter morning alone

holiday/stores closed/radio static/television
busted/only tiny blue dots/no sound/no games
scheduled/anyway/killer hangover/jack daniel's/
black rage/air sour/like butterfly/trapped/glass
jar/energy spent/seeking escape/invisible prison/
spring/lifetime away/snow drifts slowly growing
higher/old car/flat tire/brakes spongy/ominous
smoke/stink/seeping/from manifold/mouth taste/
like bird cage paper/alone/sipping warm coffee/
belly sore/ankles swollen/piss jar leak/new poems/
yellow stained/wrinkled/smelly mess/nerves shot/
fears growing/snow starting again/huge/suffocating
flakes/thinking/join brother brautigan/make/magic/
.357 poetry/finally honest/with myself.

brautigan in the yellow pages

alphabetical catchalls, "easy as abc," and convenient
miscellaneous "xyz's,"
but richard would have preferred slumming through
the neglected but important "lmno's,"
libraries, liquor, lounges, magazines, massages, mental
health, motorcycles, novelties, nurses, office supplies,
orthopedics, oxygen,
and hidden treasure, "the pumpkin tide" poem, great
riches waiting a finder, "thousands of pumpkins
bumping up against rocks and rolling up on the beaches,
reminding one the wisdom of knowing your 'lmno's,'"
pumpkins, and the times it's halloween in the sea

angling

graybeard poet's humiliation

plunging below

past record depths

brutal rejection

another young

incredibly beautiful woman

writing love poem

salving heartache

painful sense of loss

honest verse

missing femme passions

finding new lady

romance quickly finished

another another another

like brautigan's

alonzo hagen's diary

account of fishing trips made

trout lost

little sip big drink

fog bound alcatraz island

ghostly freighter shadows

passing watery straits

washington square

ianthe and her "dad"

sharing sauterne wisdom

while

bardic specter

big mac stanchions

cold icy pellets

stinging face and eyes

below

black rushing tides

somewhere

great rainbow leaping

explosive splash

trout lilies

rippling

spring in montana

snows melting absaroka summit
wild violets lower passes
eight pages
good writing morning
richard angling

mill creek "bows"
"digger dollar" billfold cache
full flask
watermelon sugar
meadow sea of daisies
we will toast nature with baitless wet
lines,
if by accident we catch a fat giant
"humpback" we'll toss him to the
soft distant clouds below

t. kilgore splake

the mountain beyond

mournful foghorn elegy

church spires vanishing

gray dying light

san francisco bay

union street hill

below washington square

brother brautigan

bench shadows

with ben franklin statue

brown sipping sack

bardic blood a-hummmm

inviting alcatraz gulls

to carry him home

musical wings

through vivaldi's "seasons"

escaping

life's surface mirror

back to absarokas

purity of motion

hiking mountain summit

moving past

thick velvety mosses

orange monarch flit-fluttering

dill pickle sardine snack

streamside nap

later afternoon shadows

soon crockpot dinner

trout onions potatoes
bardic madness stew
tender blackberries
sweet evening dessert

richard brautigan, 1984
"gentle mountain soul"

jack daniel's and big sur loneliness
savaged my good friend,
trout streams are frozen, distant troll
hut silent,
44 lead finished sensitive humor, his
intelligent wit,
deep shadows buried childhood fears,
smothered adult angsts,
"good talking candles" lay quiet, dark
curled stamens no longer a help,
he once said "the caged wolf is dead,
his journey to the moon over,"
but kind, gentle friend, the karma now
pure, your spirit still alive,
visit me in the spring on peaceful
superior shore,
with "trout fishing in america shorty"
wildflowers blooming
beginning of dawn
sustaining watermelon sugars

t. kilgore splake

chanting primal incantation
soothing bardic prayer
moving into the waterfall
beyond the rainbow

<u>brautigan's ghost</u>

nighttime collector
filling coffee can
wet wiggly nightcrawlers
early may fishing
angling girder creek trout
high waters
swift currents
after marble mountain thaw
peanut butter sandwich
big two-hearted escape
many years ago
high school diploma
during fifties conformity
school administration
closed minded principal
other students
so goddamned middle-class
no college enrollment
freshman writing classes
just academic bullshit

providing artificial safety net

off to big city life

learning to be a poet

back alley flophouse

hotel jessie room

stained kitchen sink

hot plate

tiny refrigerator

shower and toilet

down narrow hallway

scribbling found art experiences

pilot razor point pens

small green notebook

later writings

filling empty pages

lined legal tablets

using lower case

lacking punctuation skills

correct spelling never mastered

notebook clippings

scattered across wooden floor

best friend "willard"

three foot paper *mâché*owl

sitting on dresser's edge

creature of habit

each day like the past

always noting "church"

top of daily agenda

celebrating mornings

with cup of green tea
solitary poet forging art
compiling working records
"keeping yourself honest"
like old papa hem
no fallow periods
believing writer's block
excuse for second raters
writers write
talkers talk
telephone unplugged
while contesting elusive muse
failing with small presses
editors returning manuscripts
wanting mfa authors
deadly academic style
better off
producing own chapbooks
name and title
not on front covers
occasional starving artists meal
co-existence bagel shop
old spaghetti factory
smith's tea room
favorite poet's spot
window table at "the place"
menu choices on chalkboard
special movie treats
watching western "oaters"

old british murder mysteries

wearing faded jeans

black turtleneck sweater

scuffy tennis shoes

fancy neckties

wrinkled tweed jackets

cordovan brogues

alzheimer uniforms

for other people

dying of terminal ordinariness

rare days off

hitchhiking to pacific ocean

big sur picnics

flying homemade kites

visiting forgotten cemeteries

reading tombstone obituaries

names and histories

long gone

brown paper bag pints

late evenings

dreaming of flowerburgers

between toasted buns

like boho beat bum

distant voyeur

not worrying over hipness

caring for other poets

declining street jive

other writer's concerns

who's in and who's out

t. kilgore splake

important to learn about
self earth universe
varieties and dimensions
often curious
wonder if anyone listening
enjoying rare beautiful moments
when creative ideas work
things come together well
yet always remembering
peculiar sweet taste
.357 magnum metal

rosetta café

rosetta # i

woman drinking coffee
wearing sunday best
nipples tits dried up
clit untouched
pussy forgotten
distant furry sedge
rebekah circle member
saving religious promise
waiting god's grace

rosetta # ii

valentine's day
two morning hsitzzz's
married with mouths
rosetta café ethiopian
thick ceramic cups
kids long gone
husbands distant memory
alone nights
cold empty beds
middle-aged double chins
messy graying hair
thanksgiving christmas
extra holiday pounds
bullet-proofed hearts

denying love
man's hungry bones
mysterious sweet fucking
ecstatic loss of being
patrick's bran muffins
then home to watch
weather channel hours
today's special
"tornado fascination"

rosetta # iii

heavy talc dusting
white morning ghost
fresh hairdo
fancy sunday clothes
tv weather channel news
home alone pause
before rosetta coffee
looking for a friend
older children grown
living parts distant
loose wedding ring
tiny bony finger
bird-feeder filled
cat fed
no mail today
nothing to do

lacking new ideas

exciting fresh words

life a blank page

forever empty

without librium

lithium or alcohol relief

bruised self-esteem

whispers growing louder

you ought to go

back to empty house

waiting quiet death

rosetta # iv

ugly women klatch

ladies growing gray

rosetta café coffee pause

dogs waiting

in curbside gas box

chewing upholstery

no morning exercise

jeans growing tighter

new book pages unread

few "today" tv minutes

weather channel moment

exciting stories of

good people

fighting terrible storms

several tornado warnings
constant dull chatter
empty conversation
friendly feminine hugs
until next week goodbyes
home to watch
"days of our lives"
"young and restless"
brain-skull numbing soaps
until sunday's saving grace
church service with
other old farts
praising god

rosetta # v

alea alea
quiet dark-haired girl
rosetta café waitress
italian mama's daughter
her name meaning "industrious"
patrick's saturday help
serving coffee
taking breakfast orders
school rubber-stamp print
tgif gym dance proof
graybeard poet's aging dreams
bo-ho beat young romance

hard throbbing flesh

blue viagra rush

geezer rock melodies

elvis "fats" domino chuck berry

camel's twenty-three cents

pennies in cigarette machine pack

hitch-hiking rides

"on the road" miles

not flying here and there

ancient poet

creative brain-skull cavity

having to write

only few years left

before alzheimer loss

.357 trigger finger

death's shit smell

alea's boyfriend

growling tranny muffler

rusting rocker panels

foam dice rearview mirror

wearing "jock-logo" clothes

chasing fun games laughter

waiting next new craze

twitter myspace youtube facebook

wacky-tobaccy euphoria

wrinkled zig-zag papers

alea too young

to know real ghosts

believing in god

some after-life beyond

never understanding

old man on cliffs summit

imagining mysterious train below

close enough to feel

eva marie saint

cary grant

going "north by northwest"

like old steam engine

mineral range line

hauling copper ore

tamarack location

torch lake smelters

young waitress

soft gentle voice adding

"have a good weekend"

rosetta # vi

white noise morning

graying asshole

scratchy unshaven stubble

boosting self-esteem

babble-bullshitting

in cell-phone receiver

sad lonely voice

sharing his ignorance

with some other soul

not satisfied listening to

"weather on the 8's"
or checking out
early television soaper
discovering if mark
secretly took zoloft
beautiful young kim
slept with him
day quickly passing
with warm sun shining
wild birds singing
grabbing cuppa espresso
on the road refill
artful dodger companion
tranny-tripping north
to brautigan trailhead
checking autumn colors
hiking climbing
cliffs rocky path
touching tasting
quiet honest reality
red coupe curbside
sexy young man's car
rosetta café window table
decaf coffee cold
laptop steady hummm
watching cyberporn
checking stocks and bonds
new "facebook" gossip
continuous cell-phone talk

noisy voices muting
nightmare memories
of acting like dad
selfish old man
with quiet mother
lost in household shadows
friday morning
weekend without date
no nice girl
movie concert dinner
home alone again
boring television stuff
talking to himself

new poems

t. kilgore splake

<u>literary laboring</u>

graybeard busy
pressing creative envelope
running out of time
days hours minutes
focused on last writings
chasing sylvia and anne
filling notebooks
collecting new poems
before letting go

<u>time to say goodbye</u>

suddenly eighty years old
creative lifetime gone
remembering poetry books
hundreds of photographs
traveling here and there
finally giving up
one more season to run
holding childhood panda
blessed by god's wisdom
artist surrendering

well went dry

note folder closed

pens and pencils in a row

desktop squeaky clean

unwrapped legal tablet pack

poet not writing today

instead drinking alone

early morning into late afternoon

lost in demon rum ethers

waiting to feel

intelligent and successful

tempting wet-brain tremors

losing soul to darkness

hoping to drink self sober

watching tv weather channel

t. kilgore splake

<u>new blood</u>

nurse holding infant
tiny hands curled in fists
loud gutsy howl
"hey i'm here"
driving son home
riding with his mother
back of vw-bus
blanket covering face
protection against glare
boy smith's father
tightly holding steering wheel
driving very carefully
like new baby made of glass
suddenly realizing
new life waiting

truth

hesitant wannabe artist

unable to move

beyond no turning back

criticizing others

creative imagination and work

safe in absolute truths

mother flag apple pie

ignoring personal madness

pretending it doesn't happen

blind to

blood and passion

messy human chemistry

needing good life things

new tranny wheels

shiny chrome

bright enamel hues

revving wild cc's

macho harley power

expensive apartment

bayside marina view

still hungry for sex

begging girlfriend

open your legs again

quickly passing intimacy

sad soul

talking instead of writing

while fringe people

t. kilgore splake

holy kerouac ghosts

waking in beckett pages

others in arbus photos

while driven poets

chasing dreams

remembering old bukowski

having a bad day

only asking

treat me honest

becoming

early thanksgiving morning
upper peninsula solitude
facing blank page
contesting elusive muse
remembering dylan thomas
not going gently
raging against the dying light
more difficult
for graying poet
pacemaker beats
passing tia moments
fading vision
"what did you say"
facing donald hall essays
surviving the eighties
living in barcalounger
teetering walking steps
measuring daily success
getting to bathroom on time
not forgetting arthritis meds
no longer driving
without transportation
no return to brautigan creek
making final decision
knowing nursing home bed
antiseptic hospice care
unsatisfactory situation

camus' opinion on suicide
still unanswered question
still often wondering
after writing first poem
morning drinking coffee
around campfire coals
suddenly feeling real
with sense in my life
was someone or something
making invisible decision
like paul's revelation
finding the holy spirit
on the road to damascus
new creative excitement
choosing right words
making subject sing
desperately needing time
chance to see
how far i could run
escaping college captivity
dull pedantic faculty
professors without imagination
academic lifers
others trapped in society
long dreary trudge
moving from cradles to graves
driving to jobs
early morning darkness
red taillights

like bleeding arteries

precious dreams forgotten

abandoning curiosity

ignoring inner thoughts

chasing new adventures

my surprise decision

quitting serious drinking

surviving demon rum ethers·

memories recalling

john berryman's recovery

f. scott's the crackup

twenty-eight day drying out

battle creek sanitarium stay

teaching daily lectures

afternoons group therapy

 evenings professional counseling

going cold turkey

achieving sobriety

saved by mysterious power

without convulsions or d.t.s

wet-brain hallucinations

recalling suicide try

.357 barrel

between teeth and skull

oily taste on lips

childish passing moment

or decision to live

dreaming of writing companion

ray carver and tess gallagher

lively young girl

like papa hem

his "daughter" adriana

sex soon meaningless

worries undermining literary passions

realizing something forced me

to abandon youthful sex

bedroom games with someone's daughter

still pondering life's choices

fate or coincidence

my existence one wild ride

chasing exciting adventures

now recalling past

people places things

lost professor

early one morning

writing a poem

while drinking coffee

alone in the wood

<u>black kaleidoscope</u>

greybeard poet
birthday cake blazing
reaching eighth decade
enjoying golden years
tremendous lie
something never explained
kindergarten through school years
age a clever thief
can't buy back youth
relive early pleasures
chasing sexy girls
drinking to last call
eye-sight fading
slow arthritic step
heart muscle trembling
nervous hip-hop beat
no longer writing poems
memory suddenly gone
can't remember shit
refusing nursing home
depending on others
indifferent care
passing empty days
tilting .357 under chin
pointing barrel up
warm bathtub water
slow steady trickle

t. kilgore splake

letter to sheriff

tomorrow morning delivery